THE SCOOP ON POOP

POOP
Cures

by Ellen Lawrence

Consultant:
Garret Suen, Assistant Professor
Department of Bacteriology
University of Wisconsin
Madison, Wisconsin

BEARPORT
PUBLISHING

New York, New York

NUMBER TWO POO-POO POO SCAT FECES DOODY MANURE STOOL DUNG POOP DOO-DOO

Credits

Cover, © Bullstar/Shutterstock and © Steve Gschmeissner/Science Photo Library; 4L, © ARTSILENSE/Shutterstock; 4R, © Cbenjasuwan/Shutterstock; 5, © Steve Gschmeissner/Science Photo Library; 6T, © Science History Images/Alamy; 6B, © ZhdanHenn/Shutterstock; 7, © National Geographic Creative/Alamy; 8T, © Marina Shanti/Shutterstock; 8B, © joannawnuk/Shutterstock; 9, © Science History Images/Alamy; 10T, © ARZTSAMUI/Shutterstock; 10B, © Africa Studio/Shutterstock; 11, © Ian Dagnall/Alamy; 12, © Roger Viollet/Getty Images; 13, © Frans Lemmens/Getty Images; 14, © Sebastian Kaulitzki/Shutterstock; 15, © sippakorn/Shutterstock; 16, © sciencepics/Shutterstock; 17, © Steve Gschmeissner/Science Photo Library; 18, © Public Domain; 19, © Louise Murray/Science Photo Library; 20, © God is Love/Shutterstock; 21, © enmyo/Shutterstock; 21R, © Mitsuaki Iwago/Minden Pictures/FLPA; 22, © Elliott Kreloff/Shutterstock, © Virinaflora/Shutterstock, and © Tupungato/Shutterstock; 23TL, © Science History Images/Alamy; 23TC, © royaltystockphoto/Shutterstock; 23TR, © ATGImages/Shutterstock; 23BL, © sciencepics/Shutterstock; 23BC, © Pictorial Press Ltd./Alamy; 23BR, © Africa Studio/Shutterstock.

Publisher: Kenn Goin
Editor: Jessica Rudolph
Creative Director: Spencer Brinker
Photo Researcher: Ruth Owen Books

Library of Congress Cataloging-in-Publication Data

Names: Lawrence, Ellen, 1967– author.
Title: Poop cures / by Ellen Lawrence.
Description: New York, New York : Bearport Publishing, [2018] | Series: The
   scoop on poop | Includes bibliographical references and index.
Identifiers: LCCN 2017017999 (print) | LCCN 2017025670 (ebook) |
ISBN 9781684023035 (ebook) | ISBN 9781684022496 (library)
Subjects: LCSH: Traditional medicine—Juvenile literature. |
   Medicine—History—Juvenile literature. | Feces—Juvenile literature. |
   Animal droppings—Juvenile literature.
Classification: LCC GR880 (ebook) | LCC GR880 .L39 2018 (print) | DDC
   615.8/8—dc23
LC record available at https://lccn.loc.gov/2017017999

For more information, write to Bearport Publishing Company, Inc., 45 West 21st Street, Suite 3B, New York, New York 10010. Printed in the United States of America.

10 9 8 7 6 5 4 3 2 1

Contents

What's the Scoop? 4

Blood and Dung. 6

A Different Drug Store 8

Poop Powder 10

A Dose of Camel Dung 12

Hungry Bacteria. 14

The Good and the Bad 16

An Unusual Treatment 18

Poop Cures Work! 20

Science Lab 22

Science Words 23

Index 24

Read More 24

Learn More Online 24

About the Author 24

What's the Scoop?

It's brown, slimy, stinky, and everybody produces it—poop!

Poop, or feces, is made up of water and leftover food.

It also contains tiny living things called **bacteria**.

It might seem that poop couldn't be useful at all.

However, throughout history, this yucky stuff has actually been used to treat illnesses!

Can you guess which of the following were used in ancient Egyptian medicines?

worm's blood   donkey dung   dead mice

human feces and bacteria seen under a microscope

bacteria

feces

A person's **digestive system** is home to trillions of bacteria. As feces forms, lots of bacteria end up in the poop.

Blood and Dung

Around 5,000 years ago, doctors in ancient Egypt made many kinds of medicines and **ointments**.

The ingredients included dead mice, moldy bread, and poop!

To treat an infected wound, a doctor made a cooling ointment.

The recipe called for willow leaves, fat from a goat, and ox poop.

A splinter was treated with worm's blood and donkey dung.

a record of ancient Egyptian cures

Ancient Egyptian doctors kept records of their cures. Today, no one can say if these treatments helped patients get better. They may have made patients feel worse!

An ancient Egyptian doctor checks his records while treating a patient.

7

A Different Drug Store

In **medieval** times, people didn't go to drug stores for medicines.

Instead, they visited a shop run by an **apothecary**.

An apothecary made potions from plants, spices, and some odd ingredients.

To cure a chest infection, an apothecary made medicine using dog feces.

A sore throat treatment could include honey and the dried poop of children!

honeycomb

plants

Did medieval sore throat medicine look like this?

a medieval apothecary's shop

The cures for sale at a medieval apothecary's store might also contain crow droppings, human blood, pig urine, and ear wax!

Poop Powder

In the 1600s, a scientist named Robert Boyle tried to cure an eye condition called **cataracts**.

His idea was to dry human feces and crumble it into a powder.

Then the powder was blown into the patient's eyes!

Unfortunately, the poop powder did not cure cataracts.

Yet Boyle never stopped his investigations.

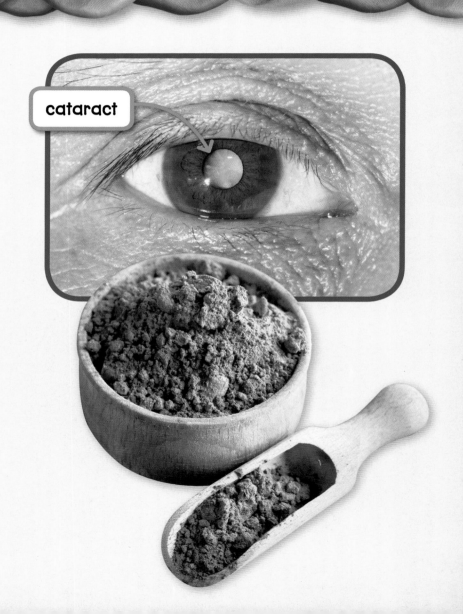

cataract

A Dose of Camel Dung

In the 1940s, German soldiers in Africa learned about a helpful poop cure.

Many soldiers were getting sick with dysentery, which causes stomach pains, diarrhea, and vomiting.

Doctors from Germany came to help the soldiers.

The doctors noticed that when local Arab people caught dysentery, they ate camel dung.

The disgusting remedy worked!

German soldiers stationed in Africa

Hungry Bacteria

The German doctors discovered that camel dung contains a very hungry type of bacteria.

Once this bacteria is inside a person's stomach, it eats the bacteria that causes dysentery.

The doctors put some of the hungry bacteria in a special soup.

Then the soldiers could get their cure without having to eat yucky poop!

The hungry bacteria found in the camel dung is called *Bacillus subtilis*. The bacteria dies soon after leaving the camel's body. That's why only fresh, warm dung can cure dysentery.

a picture of *Bacillus subtilis* created on a computer

The Good and the Bad

In a person's digestive system are trillions of good and bad bacteria.

The good bacteria help break down food and fight off the bad bacteria that cause illnesses.

Some people suffer from a serious stomach illness known as *C. diff.*

These people don't have any good bacteria in their digestive systems.

Doctors have discovered a way that poop can help. How?

C. diff is short for *Clostridium difficile.*

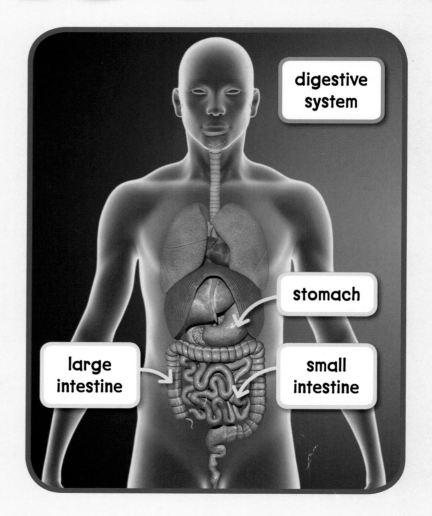

digestive system

stomach

large intestine

small intestine

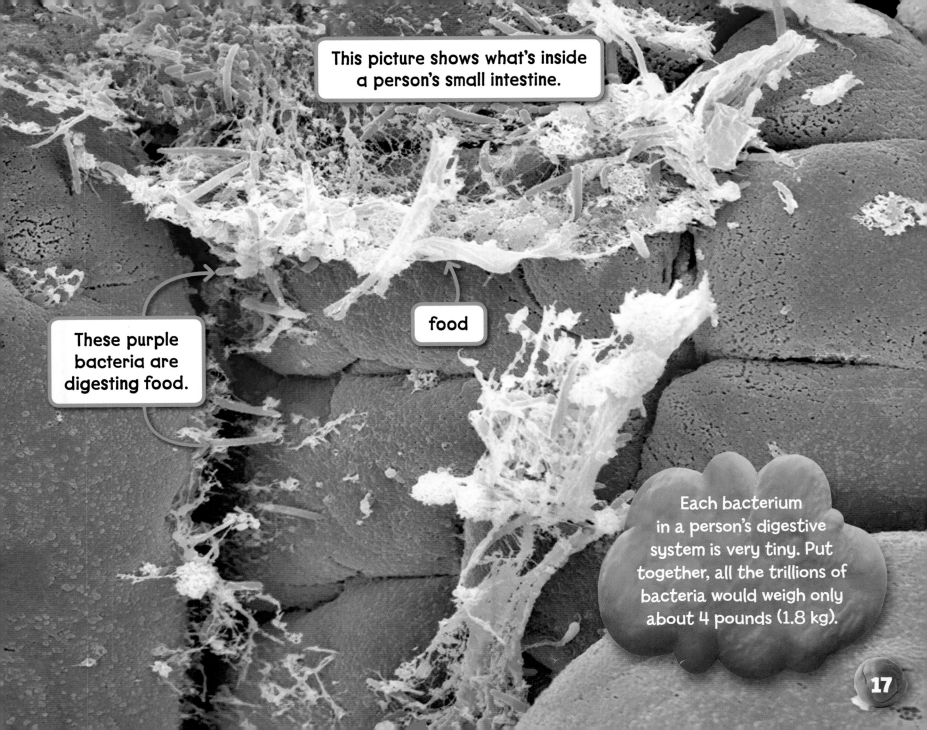

An Unusual Treatment

To help a patient with *C. diff,* a doctor takes feces from a healthy person.

The feces must contain lots of good bacteria.

Then the doctor puts the feces into the sick person's bottom using a special tube.

This treatment is called a fecal transplant.

The good bacteria then spread into the ill person's digestive system.

Li Shizhen

In the 1500s, a Chinese doctor named Li Shizhen (LEE SHEE-zen) invented a drink called yellow soup. He mixed poop from a healthy person with water. Then a patient with a stomach illness drank the poopy soup!

Poop Cures Work!

Lots of sick people have been cured by fecal transplants.

Scientists have also made a pill that contains a tiny amount of healthy poop.

A patient swallows the pill to get the good bacteria they need.

Having another person's poop in your body might sound gross, but it can work!

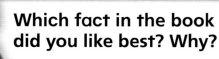

Which fact in the book did you like best? Why?

mother panda

Some baby animals are born without the bacteria they need in their stomachs. So, they eat a little of their mother's poop to get good bacteria. Elephants, rhinos, pandas, and koalas all do this.

panda poop

panda cub

Science Lab

Invent a Poopy Cure!

Pretend you are a medieval apothecary. Just for fun, make up a cure that includes poop and other odd ingredients.

Think about these questions:

What illness does your medicine or ointment cure?

How does the patient take their cure?

Write a recipe for your medieval cure. Draw pictures of your ingredients, too.

A Medieval Cure to Kill Head Lice

100 rabbit droppings
1 pint (.05 l) of pig urine
2 onions (chopped)
3 chili peppers (chopped)

Instructions
1. Put the ingredients into a pot.
2. Boil the mixture until the rabbit poop melts.
3. Let the mixture cool and then spread it on the patient's hair.
4. Leave the cure on the patient's head overnight and then wash it off.

Science Words

apothecary (uh-POTH-ih-kare-ee) a person from the past who made medicines from plants and other ingredients

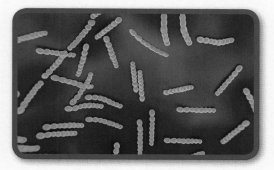

bacteria (bak-TEER-ee-uh) extremely tiny living things, such as germs, that can only be seen with a microscope

cataracts (KAT-uh-rakts) cloudy films that grow on a person's or animal's eyes and can cause blindness

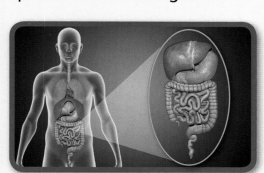

digestive system (dye-JESS-tiv SISS-tuhm) the stomach and other organs in a body that break down food

medieval (meh-DEE-vuhl) in Europe, the period in history that lasted from about the years 400 to 1500

ointments (OINT-mihnts) thick liquids or creams that are rubbed on the body to soothe pain or fight infections

Index

ancient Egyptian medicine 4, 6–7
apothecary 8–9, 22
Bacillus subtilis 14
bacteria 4–5, 14, 16–17, 18, 20–21
Boyle, Robert 10–11
camel dung 12–13, 14–15
cataracts 10
Clostridium difficile 16, 18
dysentery 12, 14
fecal transplants 18–19, 20
human digestive system 5, 14, 16–17
human poop 5, 18–19, 20
panda poop 21
Shizhen, Li 18

Read More

Canavan, Roger. *You Wouldn't Want to Live Without Bacteria!* New York: Scholastic (2015).

Farndon, John. *Strange Medicine: A History of Medical Remedies (The Sickening History of Medicine).* Minneapolis, MN: Lerner (2017).

Rake, Jody S. *Why Rabbits Eat Poop and Other Gross Facts about Pets.* Mankato, MN: Capstone (2012).

Learn More Online

To learn more about poop cures, visit **www.bearportpublishing.com/TheScoopOnPoop**

About the Author

Ellen Lawrence lives in the United Kingdom. Her favorite books to write are those about nature and animals. In fact, the first book Ellen bought for herself, when she was six years old, was the story of a gorilla named Patty Cake that was born in New York's Central Park Zoo.